How to Make Money on Amazon:
Brendan Mace's No BS Guide to Amazon

Brendan Mace

Table of Contents

Introduction

Congratulations on downloading the book 'How to Make Money on Amazon: Brendan Mace's No BS Guide to Amazon.' This book contains proven steps and strategies on how to build a passive income on Amazon.

There are many ways of making money online. The problem is most of these methods are outdated and some will require you to risk your hard earned cash on unguaranteed returns. All too often, many of the cash "opportunities" available online are run by scammers. So, how can you really make clean money online?

One of the most promising ways of making good money online is through Amazon. You may have heard of Amazon or even purchased something from the platform. What you might not have known is that you can earn money through Amazon right from the comfort of your own home either on a full time or a part-time basis.

Here's an inescapable fact: you will learn much faster from the pros how to make money through Amazon. This is what this book is all about. The goal is to educate you on the different ways you can make money online through Amazon. This book is a step-by-step guide to help every step of the way from setting up an account to making good money from it.

It's time for you to become an Amazon seller. Are you ready to start earning money online? I bet you are. Let's get started.

Free Bonus

As a thank you for taking the time to download this book, I'd like to offer you a FREE BONUS.

The free bonus is a video that shows you exactly how to create an Amazon site from scratch that makes $867.25/month.

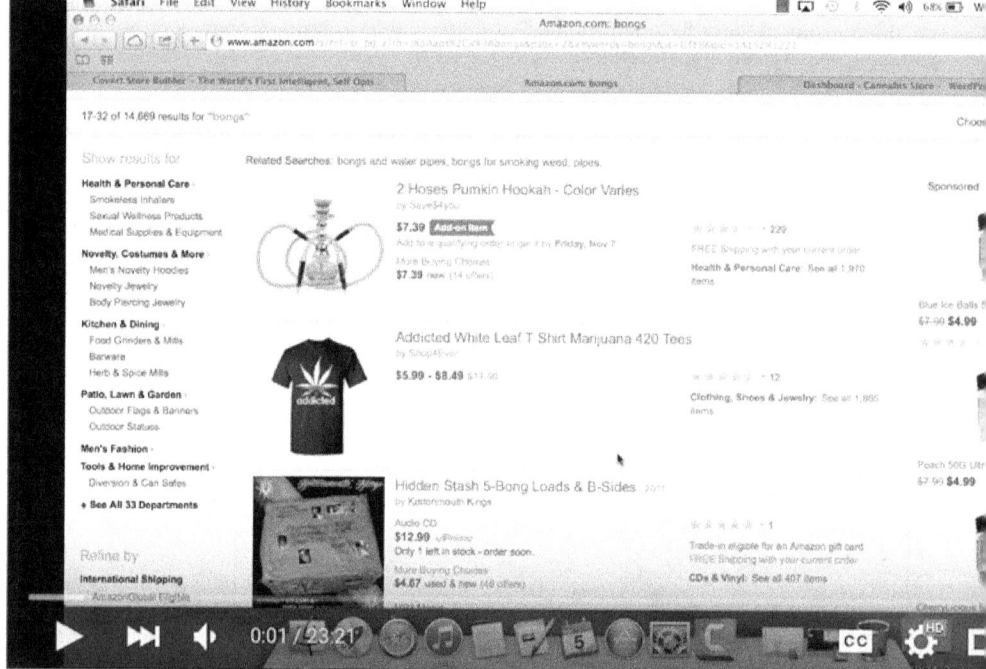

You can watch the video here:
http://twostep.brendanmace.com/amazon-video/

You'll see the theme I use to supercharge my results, and the easiest way to get going with Amazon today, and actually get results.

It won't cost you anything, so it's a no brainer to watch. Get it HERE.

Chapter 1: A Brief History of Amazon

You are eager to make money, I get that, but prior to getting started, it is important that you learn more about the platform that will help you make a living.

Jeff Bezos founded Amazon back in 1994.It is based in Seattle, Washington and is today the largest online-based retailer in the U.S.

The original home of Amazon was in Bezo's garage. However, on realizing his books were selling to buyers across the United States, Bezos realized its potential to expand across the United States. He created a website that offers a wider range of items. Once book selling was established, he diversified to CDs, DVDs, computer software, household items, toys and many more items.

Within no time, larger retailers like Target, Old Navy and Toys R Us started signing up to sell their products using the Amazon platform. This gave Amazon a greater opportunity to expand its offerings and it opened up to more product categories.

Today, Amazon has over 30 different product categories and has more than 36 million products listed; not counting the books. This offers remarkable opportunities to reach buyers and start making money on Amazon. You can tap into this and start earning.

The FBA Program

The hardest part about making money selling products online is the part of packing, shipping and fulfilling all orders. This step is labor-intensive and often pushes even the most enthusiastic of sellers to the wall. How do you meet all your customer needs and make sure the products they order get to them in the right condition? Most ecommerce sites do not do enough to shield you, the seller, from this part. However, Amazon has come up with a program that will make it easy for you.

This program is known as the Amazon's Fulfillment by Amazon (FBA) program. It is one of the things that make amazon one of the best platforms to use when you want to make money online.

The FBA program revolves around the acquisition or production of items that can be sold via the Amazon website. While your work will be finding the best products to sell and setting the right prices, Amazon will take care of storage and distribution of your products and customer service. The program gives you more free time to focus on increasing sales.

The FBA program is not something new. Over the years, Amazon has been building warehouses and distribution centers across the United States. This has been done to ensure superior customer service especially when it comes to product delivery. The service is cost-effective, fast and at times free. As a result of this efficiency, sellers consider the FBA program to simplify their work.

As you consider making money with Amazon, it is important that you consider this program. It will help you take advantage of the extensive facilities of Amazon, as well as outsource the packing, shipping and fulfillment part of your business effectively. FBA is the future of online retail and it is here.

In the following chapters, we will look at how you can make money using different methods. However, if you will choose the option that requires you to sell tangible products, you must consider using the FBA program

Different Ways of Making Money

Just an overview, with Amazon, you will have many ways to make money. The first option is by selling your products. One of the most attractive features provided by Amazon is the multi-level ecommerce.

Multilevel ecommerce

Amazon lets you sell almost anything directly through their platform. You can sell products on Amazon or sell products listed by third-parties. Simply put, Amazon is the ultimate platform for selling merchandise online.

Affiliate programs

Affiliate programs offer yet another amazing way to make money on Amazon. Here, you earn a commission through the click-through sales. You can even build an entire website based on the Amazon platform to create a mini Amazon website. With this option, you pull products right from Amazon, write your own recommendations and guides and earn a cut from the sale.

Now that you know a little about Amazon and how it works, let us take a look at some of the ways you can make money. In the next chapter, we will focus on the most important part; setting up your Amazon account.

Chapter 2: Setting up an Amazon Account

The first step to making money on Amazon is setting up your seller account. The process is relatively straightforward but you have to setup your account properly if you wish to succeed.

What is the Amazon Sellers Account?

This is the account that helps you sell products on the Amazon marketplace. The account will also help with shipping, listing orders, storage and customers service. Simply put, Amazon does all the work for you but you need this account to enjoy the benefits.

One of the best things about setting up your Amazon Sellers Account is that you will make use of Amazon's huge marketplace of buyers. You don't need to search for your own buyers.

You will have two options when setting up your account on Amazon. The options depend on the type of account you select, individual and professional. To earn big on Amazon, you should opt for the Professional account.

Why a Professional Sellers Account?

The individual account is free whereas the professional account attracts a monthly fee. Do not be tempted to go with the free account especially when considering you have already paid a lot of money for inventory and shipping fees. There are many reasons why you should opt for the professional account.

• Unlimited amount of products

With the free individual account, you can only sell a maximum of 40 items per month. This will not suit your financial plans. To make more money, you need to sell more items per month. The professional account allows you to do that. It gives you the freedom of selling as many items as you want.

• Avoid the fee per item sold

The free account will charge you an extra $0.99 per every item sold. This is in addition to other fees such as storage fees and FBA fees. The fee will eat at your profit margins. The professional account will help avoid this fee.

• Access more categories to sell in

You only access 20 different categories with the free account. This limits your options in regards to the products you can sell. The professional account will help you access 35 different categories. This might not seem like much but it surely is.

The free account is designed for persons who are just starting their retail arbitrage. Your goal is to make good money and probably quit your day job, right? Then what you need is the professional sellers account. Yes the monthly fee is unattractive but it is a necessary evil. The monthly fee is just $40 and you don't pay for the first month.

With the account type out of the way, it is time to setup your professional sellers account.

Setting up a Professional sellers account on Amazon

1. Go to http://services.amazon.com/content/sell-on-amazon.htm

The link will take you to a page where you can select to sign-up for individual or professional account. Select the '**Sell as a Professional**'. This will take you to a page where you will either sign in or create a new account.

2. Signup or sign in

If you already have an account with Amazon, all you need to do is sign-in. However, if this is the first time you are setting up an account or need a new one, select '**create a new account**'.

On the resulting page, enter your legal name and read and accept the user agreement. There are different agreements for persons not based in the United States. Once you are done, click '**Continue**'.

3. Fill the seller information

The next step is to fill out the seller information. Fill information on brand name, country, address, phone number, type of products and other required and relevant fields.

While filling out the sign-up form, make sure you pick a display name wisely. This will be your brand. Although you can change it later on, it is wise to retain the same brand name.

You should also be careful when it comes to the main product category. This is the products you plan on selling per month. Though this field is optional, you should consider filling it up. If asked if you own the brand, say '**yes**'. If you are labeling a product and selling it as your own, you need also to say '**yes**'. Only the retail arbitrages say 'no'.

4. Add a credit card to file

You need to input a debit card or credit card information. Amazon will charge the card for the monthly fees. This information will also be used to verify your identity.

5. Verify identify

Although the credit card or debt card you add will be used to verify your identity, Amazon will also require phone verification. This is done by call or text. It only takes a few minutes.

6. Tax information

In the next step, Amazon will need proper tax records. This is done using a '**Tax Interview Wizard**'. The interview is not live so take your time. The wizard will guide you through the process. Follow the instructions and you will be done within no time.

You will also need to choose how you wish to be taxed through Amazon. Creating an LLC in your state and using that business for selling products on Amazon is highly recommended. Choose LLC and select S-corporation. Fill out the EIN number and proceed.

Still on tax information, you will be required to fill the W-9 form and sign it electronically.

7. Your account is set

Filling out the tax information is the final step. Your professional sellers account is ready. You can now start selling.

Your account is now set. However, before you start selling, you will have to bear with me a little longer. We can't just jump into selling. First, we need to learn how to find the best products to sell on Amazon. We will look at this in the next chapter.

Chapter 3: How to Choose Profitable Products

To make money on Amazon, you will have to work with products that are profitable. These are products that sell fast and give you fair profit margins.

Picking a good product is definitely one of the most important factors that determine your success on Amazon. The products you select will control everything right from what your business is about to how much money you make each month.

Let's be realistic, if you pick a bad product, no matter how hard you try to sell it, most people will skip the buyer's cart. Pay attention to the reputation of a product before picking it. You must also check to see if it is something you can sell fast or something that only sells once in a while.

Checklist for profitable products

With a rough idea of how important picking a good product is, it is time to learn how to actually pick a profitable product. You need a product that can sell and sell real fast.

The following checklist will help find the product that will earn you good money and consistently.

- The product should have an average sale price of between $10 and $50. This price range encourages impulse buying.
- It should be lightweight. No more than 3 pounds. The weight will affect the shipping cost. It is cheaper to ship lightweight products.
- Similar products have 5000 best seller rank. This rating will ensure there are enough buyers to buy your products.
- There should be no brand names within the product category or niche. This will keep you from competing with brand names when selling your products.
- The item should be simple and not brittle. The item you sell should be durable, generic, specific to a single job, and is easy to use.
- The product can be made for 25% of the sale price. This will help estimate your profit margins easily.
- Top product keywords search. If the product you select gets more than 100,000 monthly searches, then this is a great product. There is adequate demand to help you make good money from it.
- It should be a year-round seller and not a seasonal seller.
- Similar products are being sold on eBay. If similar products are being sold on other sites like eBay; that is a good sign that there is demand for that item.
- Makes a better choice over similar products on the market
- It encourages recurring purchases

Brainstorming potential good products

With the knowledge of what you should look for in a product, it can be difficult to brainstorm potential products to sell. There are no solid instructions for you to follow when choosing a good product. It is up to you to test and retest until you find the perfect item for your online business.

There are certain methods you can use to make your work easier.

1. Use the Amazon Best Seller Lists

This will help you see products that are selling well and if your target product has any potential. You can find information on this through http://www.amazon.com/Best-Sellers/zgbs.

On this page, you can review categories and sub-categories to find what you really like. All in all, there are certain categories you should avoid. They include the following:

- Appstore
- Appliances
- Clothing
- Books
- Gift cards
- Electronics
- Kindle Store
- Grocery and Gourmet Food
- Software
- Shows
- Movies and TV
- Music
- MP3 downloads
- Video games
- Prime Pantry

Save for the aforementioned categories, the rest work well for private label products.

2. eBay Categories

To determine the demand of your product, make use of the eBay categories. You can access this through http://www.ebay.com/sch/allcategories/all-categories. Search different categories to find best-selling products.

3. Search Alibaba Products

Alibaba features more products that you may not have seen on Amazon and eBay. The best thing about using this option is that you will find a product that you are guaranteed there is a supplier for. You can access Aliaba through http://www.alibaba.com/Products.

Some of the best categories on Alibaba include:

- Health & beauty
- Gifts, sports & toys
- Bags, shoes & accessories
- Machinery, Industrial Parts & Tools
- Home, lights & construction

Click on the subcategories for more ideas.

4. Google Keyword Planner

This is definitely an unconventional method of finding good products to sell on Amazon. Although this method is not as good as the three aforementioned ones, it is useful. With the products you found interesting through the former methods, use Google's Keyword Planner to search for related keywords/ products.

5. Consider Your Everyday Life

This is more of an exercise to help pick the best products. What do you like? What do you use or buy on a regular basis?

The goal here is to think about what you spend most of your money on when shopping. This will give you some idea for a great product.

Tips for Verifying the Demand for a Product

You now know how to find a good product, let's take some time to learn how to verify the demand for your selected product. There are different ways of doing this.

• Think of the Niche

Does the product fall in the passion niche? If it can be used by someone for their passion, then buyers will pay for it.

You should also consider whether people need or want the item. People spend more money on items they feel they really need. Therefore, if the item is in the 'need' category, it is a great choice.

• Does it have year-round demand?

This is a very important question you need to answer. If your product is only purchased during winter, it will not be a very profitable one. This is because its demand is dependent on the season. Make use of **Google Trends** to determine whether your selected product is seasonal.

Other methods you can use to determine the demand of a product include the following:

- Amazon's Best Seller Rank.
- Number of units that sell on eBay.
- Monthly Google searches (Google Keyword Planner). The more the searches the higher the demand.
- Merchantwords.com

Enough said, let us now learn how to make real money on Amazon. Scroll to the next chapter.

Chapter 4: Listing Your Items on Amazon

You know what you need to sell. It is time to get these items listed on Amazon for you to start making money. One point you have to remember now that you are using the FBA program is that you have to manage your inventory according to the boxes. This is easy if you are only sending one box.

Every time you send a new box, you have to list the content in the box. This helps Amazon's employees to unpack, sort and shelve the items easily and accurately. There are a couple of steps you have to take when creating and listing your boxes.

1. Sign in to your seller's account and head to the Inventory menu. Select the '**Add a Listing**'.

2. Enter the name of the product you plan on selling and click on the 'Search' button. It is also possible to search under different criteria like ASIN, UPC, EAN or ISBN.

3. Select the correct choice by clicking on the 'Sell Yours' button.

4. On the next page, fill out the required information. This will include the condition of the item, price and quantity. To ensure that it is an FBA item, select the option of '**I want Amazon to ship and provide customer service for the items if they sell**'. Click Save and then Finish.

5. New sellers may see a page that requires them to confirm that the products they are selling are not hazardous, prohibited by law or capable of killing someone and so on. After that, click on the 'Send Inventory' button to proceed.

6. In this page, Amazon will require information on where you will be shipping from. You can change the default address by clicking on 'Change Address'.

7. Inform Amazon that you will be sending several items packed in a single box. If this is what you are doing, deselect the 'Individual Items' option and select the 'Case-Packed Items'. Fill out the form accordingly.

8. In the next step, Amazon will pick a facility that you need to ship your items to. You will be required to name your shipment. A generic name generated by FBA will then be issued. You can change this name if you want. Click save and continue.

9. If you have more items to add, you will have to follow steps one to eight for every item. You can also add an item to an existing shipment without having to create a new one.

Once the last item has been added, click on '**Work on Shipment**'. This will initiate the shipping process. Confirm your entries are correct before clicking on Save and then Continue. This will send you to the labeling page where you can print your labels for all the sent items. Attach these labels to your items then click Save and Continue.

Here, you can select the size of your shipment and the carrier you want to use. You can use any carrier or the Amazon-Partnered Carrier: UPS. Using UPS helps get a label at a lowered price. UPS is the easiest way to ship to Amazon. Click Save and Continue.

It is time to print the packing slips. You must note that one of the slips will need to be attached to the box. You may also need to keep a slip for yourself. Print the slips then hit Continue.

The next page requires you to give the dimensions of your boxes and weight. Save the information and click the 'Cost Estimate' button. This will give you a shipping estimate. If you agree to the quoted amount, click Accept Changes and Continue.

Print the label and attach it to the box as directed. Schedule pickup with your preferred carrier or drop the package at the nearest shipping facility.

Your product is now listed on Amazon and ready to be sold.

In the next chapter, we will look at some of the cons of using the FBA, inventory issues and costs you should be prepared for.

Chapter 5: A Look at the Cons of FBA

As you may already have figured out, making money on Amazon is pretty easy when compared with other platforms. With the FBA program, you don't need to concern yourself with packaging, shipping and customer service; all that is done for you by Amazon. All in all, before you rush into things, there are a couple of things you need to know.

Cons of FBA

Earlier in this book, we looked at the benefits of using the FBA program. However, this program is not without some downsides. It is important that you familiarize yourself with these cons before setting up.

• Not ideal for cheap items

One thing you will notice with the FBA program is that it is not ideal when you are selling cheap items like DVDs and books. If you cannot get at least $4 for your product, there is not a lot of benefits you will get with this service. Luckily, Amazon lets you know how much you stand to make once you sell a product. You will hence be well informed prior to officially sending and item in.

• Restrictions on what can be sold

It is important to note that you cannot sell just anything on Amazon. There are also some restrictions on how to sell and what to sell. For example, Amazon will require that you package your products in a certain way to assist them with adding them into the system. If you miss an ISBN or a bar code, you will have difficulty adding the item into the Amazon system.

• Can be frustrating at the beginning

When you start using the FBA, you might find the process frustrating. However, as you get used to it, it will be easy.

The three are the main disadvantages of using FBA. We will not talk about the monthly fee since this is just a necessary evil. There are, however, a couple more things you need to consider.

Be ready for damaged or returned items

Amazon is one of the leading ecommerce sites because of its superior return policy that favors consumers. The number one priority of Amazon is to keep customers happy. Consequently, buyers can return items for absolutely any reason. One of your buyers will inevitably abuse this policy. If you realize you are getting too many returns, the product you are offering is probably the problem.

Another thing you have to understand is that although Amazon handles the packaging and shipping, you are still responsible for the item. If the product arrives to the buyer being less than perfect, it may be returned and you will bear the cross.

The important fact to bear in mind here is that at least 3 to 5% of the items you send will be returned. Some of them will be unsellable.

Amazon Competition

When you join Amazon and start selling, you may enjoy a certain level of monopoly. Unfortunately, other sellers will copy you and your honeymoon will be short-lived. The important point to remember is that you are not only competing with third-party merchants but also with Amazon itself. Amazon is pricing similar products at the same price or lower, can you keep up? You will only enjoy a peace of mind if you offer a product that is not offered by Amazon.

Inventory Issues

Several inventory issues may arise when using FBA. They include:

- **Unfulfillable inventory**. This happens when a customer returns an item. Amazon will determine whether the returned item can be resold or not. If it can be resold, it will be added to your FBA inventory but if it cannot, it will fall under unfulfillable. When this happens, the item can either be returned to you or destroyed.

  It is recommended to remove all unfulfillable inventories on a monthly basis. Needless to say, these inventories will bite into your returns.

- **Missing/ lost/ damaged inventory**. Some of your inventory may be unaccounted for at one point in time. This could be a serious delay or actual loss. If Amazon damaged or lost your inventory, you will be compensated.

Costs to take note of

- **Commission**. Through its program, Amazon takes a commission on all sales. The important thing is to ensure you can live with the cut. If the commission affects your profits significantly, it may not be worthwhile.
- **Additional fees**. You have to account for extra fees that may creep up. The commission is not always straight. Certain fees to consider include item pickup fees, handling fees, fees based on weight of items, Long Term Storage system fees and so on.
- **Advertising costs**. Your willingness to pay for advertising on Amazon will significantly affect your success. However, using this service may attract a substantial price tag. Weigh the pros and cons carefully before signing up.
- **Shipping costs**. You are responsible for the costs of shipping your items to Amazon.

The FBA offers a convenient option for sellers to leverage on Amazon's popularity, resources and solid reputation to increase their marketplace sales. The program is ideal for both individuals and businesses trying to change and expand their reach in the dynamic market of ecommerce. The Fulfillment program by Amazon offers a great alternative to the traditional modes of selling online.

So far, we have been looking at the different ways of making money on Amazon by selling products through the FBA program. But what if you don't want to sell tangible products? In the next chapter, we are going to focus on other different ways of making money other than selling items.

Chapter 6: Making Money Using the Affiliate Program

Amazon was designed to be a platform for selling products online. However, this is not the only way you can make money on here. One of the most promising alternatives to selling tangible products on Amazon is making use of the Amazon affiliate program.

Amazon Associates

If you have a website or a blog, affiliate marketing is one of the best ways to make extra money on Amazon. This is thanks to the Amazon affiliate program that is known as Amazon Associates. The program allows you to make 4% or even more on all purchases that are made using special links on your website or blog.

To benefit from the Amazon affiliate program, there are a couple of things you need to do.

1. Start an Online Effort

Some of the best Amazon Affiliates are the bloggers and website owners that add links to Amazon as well as quality content. If you don't already have a website or blog, you can use my Hostgator coupon code: '**get25offyourbill**'.

To start making money with the affiliate program, you should consider one or all of the following.

- Start a blog. You can start a free blog with WordPress, Blogger or any other similar site. Choose a niche you are passionate about and start adding interesting content and work on developing a following.
- Create a website. A business or professional website can use Affiliate programs and start earning you extra money. All in all, this will only work best if you don't sell similar products on your site. This is because the Amazon marketplace can easily drive your business away. Other than that, if you have a website that promotes different products, non-profit, club or any other service; you can recommend products on your website and make money.
- Set up a social media account. You can setup multiple social media accounts for your website or blog. This will improve your search engine ranking, connect you intimately with your audience and increase the number of links you share. It is okay to share the Amazon links on Twitter, Facebook or LinkedIn. This will be effective when you want to make recommendations.

2. Post Quality Content

Your success when using the affiliate program will depend on the size of your following. Needless to say, the best way of creating a large and loyal following is to always provide your audience with quality content that adds value to their lives. Resolve to post fresh content at least once every week.

To gain loyalty, your content should not just pitch to your customers. Make your content fun and educative. If you are only pushing your visitors to click on your links and buy products on Amazon, you will lose them.

Sign up for Amazon Associates

Now that your website or blog is up and running, it is time to sign up for the Amazon Associates. You do this by going to affiliate-program.amazon.com. Make sure you read the information on this page before you sign up. The information will let you know which products are eligible, how you should post and how you will get paid.

With the Amazon Associates, you get paid based on advertising fees or commissions. The rate varies depending on the product you are advertising. If you refer over 6 purchases each month, the advertising fees may go up. This means you will make more money.

After reading and understanding the information provided, click on '**Join Now for Free**'. Sign in with your Amazon username & password. You should also select the official payment address from here or add one.

After you sign in, you will have to fill out important information about your website, your web traffic as well as online monetization. You will be required to enter all the sites that you will be using to post the Amazon links.

The next thing you have to do is go through the products featured on the Amazon's Associated Central. Pick a couple of products to add to your blog posts. You can use the 'Bestseller' filter in order to find the products that are bestselling in all categories.

Once you find a product you like, post its link in your blog or website. You can post an image alone, an image and text or simply the text link. The choice is all yours.

You can capture the links of all the products you wish to post using the Amazon Associates site stripe. This toolbar is located at the top of the page.

How to Increase Your Amazon Associates Profits

To increase your earnings, you have to post links regularly. You have to continually search for ways to incorporate products into your posts while still offering quality content to your readers.

Once the affiliate links are clicked, they are active for 24 hours. This simply means they will expire within 24 hours. Fresh links will increase your chances of making money.

Another way of increasing your earnings is to build links to as many different types of products as you can. Your earnings are based on the total purchase made by the client you refer to Amazon and not just on the one product you were advertising.

Using referral links when sending emails or to family members will also increase your earnings. You will get a commission when anyone makes a purchase. However, you will not earn anything if you use the link yourself or if the link is not used within 24 hours.

However, if you wish to make a purchase and earn a commission, you can trade your referral link with a family member or friend. Make your purchase using the link.

Adding Amazon's widgets on your website will further boost your earnings. There are several widgets you can add to your template to list recommended products in a sidebar.

Advertising expensive products means you get a bigger commission when they are purchased. Do not shy away from items that cost more than $100.

Last but not least, you have to optimize your website. The more traffic your website gets, the more people will see your links. Search engine optimization is something you must take seriously.

In the next chapter, we will look at some unconventional ways of making money on Amazon.

Chapter 7: Unconventional Ways of Making Money on Amazon

So far, we have looked at how to sell products using the FBA program and how to earn money using the affiliate program. There are, however, a couple more methods you can use to make money on Amazon. Here are a few unconventional methods you should consider using to supplement your earnings.

1. Publish an eBook

Are you a passionate writer or knowledgeable in a certain field? You can make money by publishing your eBooks on Amazon. To do this, you need to register with Kindle Direct Publishing (https://kdp.amazon.com/). It is free to register.

This will help publish your eBook on Kindle within 5 minutes and it will appear on Kindle stores in 48 hours. Once your book sells, you earn up to 70% of the royalties. You will also keep the publishing rights and set your own price.

In addition to that, you can join the Kindle Owner's Lending Library. This enables prime members to borrow your book. They will subsequently give you more exposure.

2. Sell Original Content

You can make money by selling your original content on Amazon. For example, you can sell your content in books, DVDs, CDs. MP3s and video downloads. You can do this directly on the Amazon platform. This can be done through CreateSpace (hhttps://createspace.com/). CreateSpace is a company owned by Amazon. It pays royalties when a product is sold on Amazon.

Do you produce your own music or create your own art? CreateSpace will turn your hobby into a 'retail-ready' product with jewel case, full-color inserts and printed disc. You will also get a free UPC (Universal Product Code). The item will be sold directly on Amazon and will be eligible for the two-day delivery and great consumer exposure.

The royalties will depend on the category the product falls in. It ranges from 40% to 60% of the selling price.

3. Completing Tasks on Amazon Mechanical Turk

This is a great way to earn money during your free time. With the Amazon Mechanical Turk (https://www.mturk.com/mturk/welcome), you complete simple tasks for a decent earning. For example, you can describe images in less than 10 words for 10 cent payment. Semi-detailed product reviews will earn you $2.50.

Although most of the tasks don't pay much, the amount will add up pretty fast. You just need to be patient and search for better paying tasks.

4. Score Discounts

You can create an account on Snagshout (https://www.snagshout.com/) for free. This will give you access to extremely discounted Amazon products in exchange for honest product reviews of the products you purchase. The discounts range from 50% to almost 90% off the retail price.

With this option, you shop normally. However, when the item arrives, you will be required to give an honest review. When you do this, you gain access to other discounted items. Simply put, you are paid with extreme discounts on items you would purchase.

The four alternative ways of making money via Amazon are straightforward. They all have the potential to be lucrative when used properly.

Away from making money on Amazon, it is time to look at some of the best kept secrets. Tips that will help you earn more on Amazon.

Chapter 8: Amazon's Best Kept Secrets

Some people make more money on Amazon than others. The reason behind this is not just the wrong choice of product or strategy but how they manage their online business. Now that you have resolved to make money via the Amazon platform, you need to understand some of the best kept secrets.

1. Follow the Rules and Guidelines

Needless to say, there are rules that have been set by Amazon. You need to follow them to avoid being banned from the platform.

You have gone through the process of setting up your account, picking the best product to sell and signing up for an Affiliate program, the last thing you want is to risk being kicked off the site. This happens if you don't adhere to the rules.

2. Learn how to become an amazing seller

Amazon has a featured merchant features. This will help you be even more successful since buyers will trust you. However, there is no set formula for becoming a featured merchant. However, to increase your chances, you need to garner good feedback, have good sales, and have the right account type.

As a featured merchant, which happens a few months after proving yourself as a reliable seller, you will get a 'Buy Box'. This will give you default sales. Becoming a featured merchant on amazon will double your sales.

3. Make use of the fulfillment program

The Amazon fulfillment program is a must have. It will take the weight of packing, and shipping products off your shoulders. You will have more time to focus on growing your new business.

4. Choose products that are sited for your size of business

It will be impractical to start selling sofas and mattress right from your garage, don't you think? That is unless you have a really huge garage. The point here is to choose items that you can manage. You should also note that you may incur losses due to damages or inventory losses. Make sure a single loss will not drive your business down the drain.

5. Have a flexible pricing strategy

Setting your price too high will push customers away whereas setting it too low will reduce your earnings. Find the perfect balance. You need good margins for your business to be sustainable.

6. Go through the Seller Central Reports

To know if your business is doing well or not, you need to make use of the Amazon's Seller Central reports. These reports, found on your seller account, will show you how much you are making, how your inventory is and if people are taking advantage of promotions.

There are many more tips you can use out there. Keep learning.

Next, let us look at some of the mistakes you need to avoid.

Chapter 9: Common Mistakes to Avoid as an Amazon Seller

You now understand how to start making money on Amazon, it is time to learn of a few common mistakes you need to avoid. The purpose of this final chapter is to help you understand some of the big mistakes that sellers make.

1. Assuming Amazon's shipping rates are always accurate

If you have been on Amazon for long, then you know that these rates are not always accurate. Although the prices will go up based on the size and weight inputted, it is important to confirm that everything is accurate.

2. Forgetting to leave a review

If you have used a product or know more about it, it is important to leave a detailed review based on your experience of knowledge. Your review will help other buyers make quick decision. Give your products a fair rating of no more than 4 ½ out of 5.

3. Failing to compare prices before pricing your own

To set a competitive price for your products, you need to know how much similar products are retailing at. If your product is too expensive, buyers will choose your competitors.

Setting the price about convenience is also a great thing. In terms of convenience, we mean products that can be shipped for free.

4. Failing to market the product well

You need to market your product well if you want it to sell fast. Upload photos of the item and add a detailed description of it. Your product should look good and sound good. All in all, you must never advertise falsely.

5. Following the crowd

Yes it is good to sell something that is being sold by other sellers but that only means the competition will be stiff. Selling items that are not being sold by anyone else will give you a better competitive edge.

6. Not taking the product offline when away

How you treat their customers is what Amazon really cares the most about. If you are quick to deliver purchased items and fast in responding to messages, you will get a better rating from Amazon. Whenever you are going away, take the product offline until you get back.

7. Failing to account for occasional returns

There is a good chance that some of the products you sell will be returned for any reason. If they are returned because they are damaged, this will bite into your finances. If your items have a return policy, you have to account for returns every time you sell them.

8. Not checking your email often

When an item has been sold, you will get a notification. Make sure you check your email as often as possible. You should also not be afraid to contest bad reviews or claims.

The eight are just common mistakes you should avoid at all cost. Other than that, Amazon is the best place to make money online. You get a huge audience of buyers, a reliable system for selling and leverage on the trust factor of Amazon.

Conclusion

Thank you again for downloading this book!

I hope this book was able to help you learn how to start making money on Amazon.

The next step is for you to take action. Use this guide to setup your Amazon account, select the best product and start marketing. If you don't wish to sell products, you can make use of the affiliate programs.

Finally, if you enjoyed this book, please take the time to share your thoughts and post a review on Amazon. It'd be greatly appreciated!

Thank you and good luck!

www.ingramcontent.com/pod-product-compliance
Lightning Source LLC
Chambersburg PA
CBHW070351190526
45169CB00010B/1517